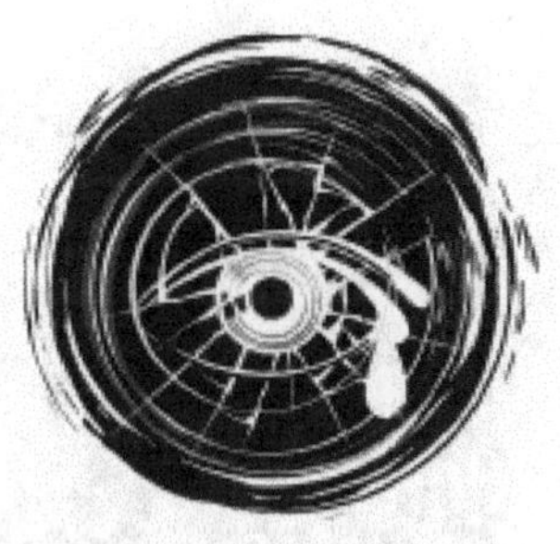

MORAL INJURY

A Deeper Insight into the Intricacies
of PTSD Among Veterans

TOM SEALS

Available online wherever books are sold.

988

SUICIDE &

CRISIS LINE

Text HOME to 741741 to connect with a volunteer Crisis Counselor.

ATTRIBUTIONS
Interior Text Font: Minion Pro
Cover Design & Typesetting: Robbie W. Grayson III

ISBN: 979-8-8693-0189-5

BOOK PUBLISHER INFORMATION
Traitmarker Books
A Division of Traitmarker Media
www.traitmarkerbooks.com
traitmarker@gmail.com

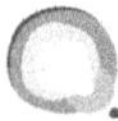

Table of Contents

A Note from the Publisher

The publisher is providing this book and its contents on an "as is" basis and makes no representations or warranties of any kind with respect to this book or its contents and disclaim all such representations and warranties, including but not limited to warranties of mental healthcare for a particular purpose.

The content of this book is for informational purposes only and is not intended to diagnose, treat, cure, or prevent any mental/social condition or disease. This book is not intended as a substitute for consultation with a licensed practitioner. Please consult with a physician or healthcare specialist regarding the suggestions and recommendations made in this book.

An Introduction to
Moral & Spiritual Injury

Did you know it is possible to be outwardly moral without being spiritually righteous? For example, when Paul came into the city of Athens and beheld all the religious idols displayed along the road from the seaport to the city, he was emboldened to say to the people in the coliseum: "I perceive that in every way you are very religious" (Acts 17:22).

While being "very religious," or a very moral people, the Athenians were susceptible to all the pagan vices that were prevalent in their various religions: cultic prostitution, idolatry, gluttony, child sacrifice, etc. In a more modern scenario, a religious fanatic might believe that it is morally right to kill all infidels—men, women, and children—who do not pattern their lives after a particular brand of religion.

Moral injury can develop because of violating one's moral code, which is a code possibly based on outward human conduct from a humanistic viewpoint. The standard of such a moral code may be according to the traditions of men, of culture, of country, and a code motivated by violation of these traditions and motivated by fear of being shunned by the community. The power behind such a morality is the power of human will and determination.

Spiritual injury, on the other hand, can develop because of violating God's moral code, as understood from the Judeo-Christian Scriptures. Right living and right activity are determined by adhering to the truths revealed in the Bible by God through God, Jesus Christ, the Holy Spirit, and the inspired writers. The goal of such a spiritual life is righteousness based on the principles of God. It is a spirituality that comes from God as the believer strives to live out the righteousness of God in daily life. The power behind such spiritual power is "Christ living in" the believer.

Tom Seals

Bellevue, Tennessee | March 2024

MORAL INJURY

The following incident was reported in *Newsweek* on December 3, 2012:

In April 2003, Fox Company, 2nd Battalion, 23rd Marines engaged the Republican Guard in Iraq. Over 5,000 rounds of ammunition were expended, along with rocket-propelled grenades being fired. Bullets flew from surrounding second story windows; glass from broken windshields pierced soft flesh. Along with all the kinds of chaos associated with such firefights, there were also IED-laden vehicles. If there was any kind of good news coming from this battle, it was the fact that all Marines in this engagement came home alive.

The resulting trauma from the battle, however, produced debilitating psychic wounds in the months succeeding in the battle. PTS(D) was rampant; one in two Marines carried with them, following this battle, debilitating psychological wounds. The Marines returning home and acclimating back into the society faced so many other kinds of re-adjustment problems, such as, joblessness, homelessness, divorce, spousal abuse, drug/alcohol dependence, and even self-induced death.

What went wrong? The answer is both simple and complex. These individual warriors had "lived through hell" and, like 300,000 other veterans, were badly shaken by the battlefield. And, like many before and after, their treatments consisted of medications, talk therapy, psychological sessions, and other attempts to heal such psychic wounds.

There are three attempts of suicide every ninety minutes (one in three successful). After three decades of research to this day, it is estimated that veterans continue to experience a suicide rate of **18 to 22 reported suicides a day.**

The history of the development of psychological trauma from exposure to events of danger to human life and well-being, known today as PTSD, has been a part of the human condition for as long as recorded history has occurred. This history predates Christ. In 1000 BCE, an Egyptian combat veteran named Hori wrote about his pre-battle experience:

"You determine to go forward... Shuddering seizes you, the hair on your head stands on end, your soul lies in your hand."

The modern terminology known as post-traumatic stress disorder (PTSD) is as old as war itself and can be traced back to antiquity. This condition was called "soldier's heart" during the Civil War in America, later to be called "shell shock" in WWI and "battle fatigue" in WWII. During the Korean conflict, this condition was labeled "operational exhaustion," later referred to as "PTSD" after Vietnam.

The American Psychiatric Association has added PTSD to its list of recognized mental disorders. This was followed by *Time* magazine reporting in 2015 that over the past 13 years as many as 500,000 US troops who served in Iraq and Afghanistan have been diagnosed with PTSD.

To address this growing disorder, partially brought on by advancement in medical care that has resulted in fewer men and women dying from once fatal combat wounds, the Department of Defense has begun extensive research into what is referred to as "moral injury." In the military culture, moral injury has typically been defined as:

- Pervasive guilt and shame

- A sense of being beyond forgiveness

- A hopeless nihilism, separation from community and creation

- An inability to render a distinction between moral right and wrong

- A failure to exhibit moral leadership.

As we examine how we might bring about healing in the lives of veterans suffering from moral/spiritual healing, we must obtain peace and hope by setting forth the possibility of grace and forgiveness.

The immediate concern here is to define the standard for determining moral injury in the military context. Moral injury is generally defined as "An act of transgression, which shatters moral and ethical expectations that are grounded in religious or spiritual beliefs, or cultural-based rules about fairness."

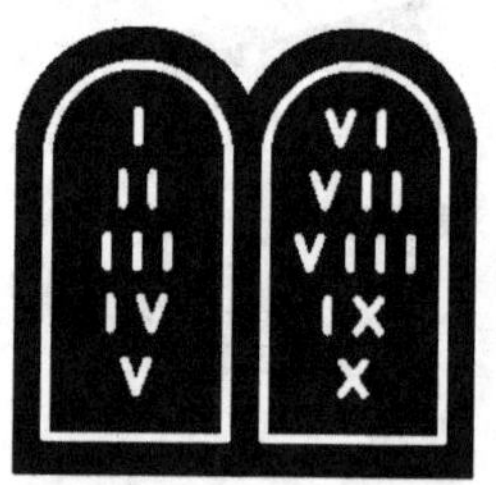

Morality is generally defined according to one's values, such as no killing, no stealing, working hard, etc., all having to do with outward conduct—*what one does!* Such a system of morality can be influenced and acquired by societal norms, one's environment, country, race, etc.

Typically, most cultures have a basic code of morality that addresses these outward failures. But what about one's inner being? What happens when one violates one's spiritual values, values of the inner being, such as pride, selfishness, lust, and so forth, things forbidden by the Judeo-Christian ethic but not necessarily cultural norms?

The problem is that such "morality" has no theological (biblical) roots.

This brings us to the aspect of spiritual injury. Spirituality is the development of foundational values based on spiritual beliefs, not just some social code. It involves being in a spiritual relationship with God and the community. It results from a spiritual relationship with God, Christ, and the Holy Spirit.

If one believes themselves to be created in the "image of God" and created to have fellowship with God, spiritual injury results when one violates that image and relationship. Such spiritual injury cannot only be cured by medication or treated with secular psychology.

An example of the difference between moral and spiritual injury is illustrated in the New Testament in the story of Paul at Athens (cf. Acts 17). When Paul entered the city, he was impressed by the number of statues to various gods that aligned the street leading from the seaport to the city. He even noticed the sincerity of the people by remarking that he had seen a statue to "an unknown God," just in case they might have missed one.

To this distinction, Paul said, "I perceive that in every way you are very religious" (Acts 17:22).

Did Paul take this expression, a "very religious" people, to indicate that they were in a right relationship with their true Creator, the Lord God of the universe? Of course not, because he goes on from this point to reveal to the Athenians this "unknown God," the God who does not dwell in statues or temples but within the inner spiritual being of every individual created in the image of this God.

The point we are making is that one can keep all the commandments, rituals, and mores of a particular religion and be found morally upright without ever addressing that inner spirit that may not be in a proper spiritual relationship with their Creator. The problem we face today is that the military feels it cannot address such spiritual aspects associated with spiritual injury. This is because spiritual injury lies deep within the inner being of Christian individuals who are focused on an awareness of a relationship with the God of the Christian faith, and the Department of Defense is not allowed to specifically address the psychic injuries from a specific Judeo-Christian vantage point. Neither medications nor secular psychology can effectively address such situations because they must be addressed from the realities of a spiritual vantage point.

In a timely article, "The Twin Wounds of War," USA Chaplain Col. Tim Mallard sets forth twelve markers resulting from spiritual injury. I add brief comments after each marker.

1. THE LOSS OF A RELATIONSHIP WITH GOD—War can strain deeply-held beliefs, forcing one to seek stronger connections with God or abandon him in despair.

2. God's Providence and/or Sovereignty—Where is God when things go "south"? If God is Omniscient, omnipresent, and omnipotent, how did such carnage, etc., happen?

3. SUFFERING—To hear another crying out in agony and pain, to witness injuries, to see shrapnel or rocket wounds, IEDs, and then have to face the family of the buddy killed often produces deliberating trauma.

4. Forgiveness—Typically, a spiritually wounded warrior is given clinical therapy, but there is a greater need than psychological jargon because the warriors may need forgiveness for what they did or did not do. Something more is needed and usually requires religious leaders to meet these needs.

5. PARALYZING DOUBT—Post-deployed veterans suffering from spiritual wounds often feel they are beyond the pale of forgiveness and unacceptable to God. Often, the warrior feels that God himself has turned against him in judgment. It can lead to a "Get me, God" attitude. This further alienates the veteran from God who is the only source of spiritual healing. One descends into a state of despair and hopelessness.

6. Excessive Sorrow—Sorrow is an appropriate response to moral tragedy. Christ grieved deeply over the human tragedies of his era (cf. Isaiah 53:3; Matthew 14:10-13; John 11:34-35; Luke 19:41-44; Matthew 26:36-46; Hebrews 5:7-9).

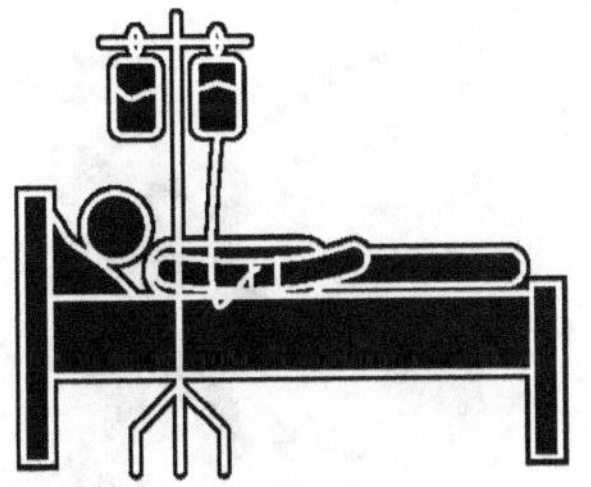

7. Justice and Reconciliation—Anger can be a good sign, for it reveals a still functioning morality that is outraged at evil and injustice, which is much better than apathy and disregard. However, there must be no revenge or retaliation urges. Then, too, there must be a reexamination of the "Just War" theory used to ensure that one's anger is proper.

8. Truth or Faith Claims—War and its resulting carnage can lead to a faltering faith and trust that may cause one to utter "blasphemous" ideas and words. This is natural (cf. Job), thus the importance of refraining from aggressively challenging a warrior's crisis of doubt.

9. Identity, Meaning, or Purpose—
After combat, there may be that question-
ing of "Who am I," "What do I do now,"
and "What is my purpose in the future?"

10. Theology of the Body—Many
warriors are surviving physical traumas
to where the ratio of "killed in action" or
"died of wounds" has dropped from the
historical trend of one in three to one in
seven. Such injuries (amputations, cata-
strophic burns, loss of sensory perception)
create questions as to the sacred nature
of human creation, what it means to be a
whole person, the possibility of intimacy,
etc. Thus, the necessity of the resurrection
hope in Christ.

11. HOPE AND ETERNAL LIFE—Warfare often produces a mood of nihilism and loss of faith in an existential hope in eternal life with God.

12. Sanctorium Communio—Warriors often suffer from a spiritual injury that produces a life devoid of any meaningful social or religious connections and relationships.

Colonel Mallard concludes his article by pointing out that contemporary war has become confusing with differing and often contradictory missions, especially in combat. Today, insurgents hide among women, children, and other non-combatants. Such situations have the strong possibility of producing ambiguous moral situations.

Finally, war is engaged in cyberspace, autonomous warfare systems, pandemics, and challenges like competition for water, arable land, and food supplies.

For example, a pilot of UAVs (drones) in Colorado Springs, CO., may work eight hours daily at a monitor. He then goes home and takes the kids to a McDonald's or a sports event and returns to work the next day. In all this, he never addresses the spiritual aspects of the damage done and what might have occurred thousands of miles away.

The result is that moral and spiritual injuries will continue to damage sensitive souls despite the changing context of war.

In such situations as this, faith communities, programs (such as God's Word for Warriors), and men and women of faith must step up and address the spiritual injuries of our warriors. To fail to do this would be to attempt to solve a bad fruit situation on a tree by replacing the fruit without going to the tree's foundation and treating the disorder with proper fertilizer.

Using medications, secular psychology, and other programs by themselves to solve the problem of spiritual injury, without addressing the spiritual condition brought on by the evils of war that our warriors witness, will continue to be unsuccessful. Medicines may reduce symptoms, but they may very well bring forth problems in other areas.

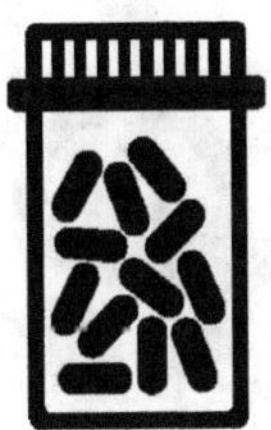

So, the prevalence of PTSD caused many veterans to face the challenge of identifying the most effective methods of treatment. There are several treatment options available, such as the following:

- Prolonged Exposure Therapy
- Cognitive Processing Therapy
- Eye Movement Desensitization and Reprocessing
- Stellate Ganglion Block

Further research on these options can be found at VA.gov under "PTSD Treatment Options." These treatment options, coupled with spiritual input from godly counselors for individuals, will go a long way in treating and developing individuals to handle such war-related spiritual wounds in their individual lives.

There are also some self-recovery pro-cesses available to those who experience PTSD. Recovery from PTSD is a multi-faceted and ongoing process. Some things that one might add to their regimen that can assist in recovering and maintaining a whole life are:

- Stay connected with family and friends. Do not self-isolate.

- Add exercise and relaxing techniques to your daily routine.

- Refrain from alcohol, drugs, and caffeine.

- Get the proper amount of sleep.

- Serve others through volunteering efforts.

In addition, families can be of great assistance in helping PTSD sufferers in the following ways:

- Educate yourself on PTSD, what to expect, and how to support it.
- Engage in conversation with other families who have experienced the same conditions as their loved ones.
- Do not take the symptoms of PTSD personally.
- Do not pressure your loved one into talking about their situation.
- Make sure the person with PTSD has one-on-one time with every family member.
- Exercise patience and understanding, avoiding judgmental statements.
- Express confidence that things will work out for the higher good if the parties work together.
- Try to recognize, anticipate, and be prepared for PTSD triggers.
- Do not let PTSD dominate your life by ignoring your own needs.

Is recovery from PTSD possible? Most studies I have read say *Yes*. I'm not there yet.

What I can say, however, is that if complete recovery is possible, it will be a gradual, complex, and ongoing process.

The thing that is so hopeful, however, is that all PTSD sufferers can learn to cope with the situation more effectively. PTSD sufferers can develop to the point where there will be fewer and less intense symptoms and better management when symptoms start to arise.

We do not have to let PTSD dominate our lives.

Recommended Readings

Dr. Tim Mallard, "The Twin Wounds of War," Providence (Winter 2018).

Keith Meador, William C. Cantrell, and Jason Nieuwsma, "Recovering from Moral Injury," Baylor University.

Dr. Thomas L. Seals, *The Quest for Spiritual Maturity,* Ch. 6, "Living the New Life," Truth Books/ CEI Books." (855) 492-6657 or (256) 206-6052

988

SUICIDE &

CRISIS LINE

Text HOME to 741741 to connect with a volunteer Crisis Counselor.

About the Author

Dr. Tom Seals served in the United States Marine Corps from 1957-1960, with the 3rd Marine Division in Okinawa, Japan, during the Laos-Vietnam era, followed by several years with the U.S. Government in Europe.

Later, he taught undergraduate Bible courses as well as Biblical ethics and textual studies for twenty-eight years at Lipscomb University in Nashville, TN, and served as Chaplain to Veterans until his December 2020 retirement. He received the diploma, Master Course in Electronics from Cleveland Institute of Electronics in 1964, his Bachelor of Arts in Biblical languages from Lipscomb University in Nashville, TN, in 1971, his Master's degree from Wesley Seminary in Washington, D.C. in 1976, and his Doctorate in Ministry from Memphis Theological Seminary in 1999. Dr. Seals later completed post-doctoral work in Pentateuchal Studies and Religion, Politics, and Social Issues from Vanderbilt University in 2008.

He has published *Proverbs: Wisdom for All Ages, Sermon on the Mount for Modern Living, The Quest for Spiritual Maturity: A Study of Dietrich Bonhoeffer's The Cost of Discipleship,* and *God's Word for Warriors.*

He has served as a pulpit minister in Virginia, Tennessee, and Colorado and is presently teaching at the Bellevue Church of Christ in Nashville, TN. Tom was actively involved with an educational ministry in Lima, Peru, serving as International President. Presently, Tom serves as Founder and President of God's Word for Warriors.

Tom and his wife, Barbara, have three children: Amy, Tom Jr. (deceased), and Melanie, along with three grandchildren.

Contact the Author

tom@godswordforwarriors.com

912 Harpeth Valley Place
Nashville, TN 37221

615.430.3544